D1480063

NORTH AMERICAN ANIMALS

# Black Bears

by Megan Borgert-Spaniol

BLASTOFF! READERS
3

BELLWETHER MEDIA • MINNEAPOLIS, MN

Note to Librarians, Teachers, and Parents:

**Blastoff! Readers** are carefully developed by literacy experts and combine standards-based content with developmentally appropriate text.

**Level 1** provides the most support through repetition of high-frequency words, light text, predictable sentence patterns, and strong visual support.

**Level 2** offers early readers a bit more challenge through varied simple sentences, increased text load, and less repetition of high-frequency words.

**Level 3** advances early-fluent readers toward fluency through increased text and concept load, less reliance on visuals, longer sentences, and more literary language.

**Level 4** builds reading stamina by providing more text per page, increased use of punctuation, greater variation in sentence patterns, and increasingly challenging vocabulary.

**Level 5** encourages children to move from "learning to read" to "reading to learn" by providing even more text, varied writing styles, and less familiar topics.

Whichever book is right for your reader, Blastoff! Readers are the perfect books to build confidence and encourage a love of reading that will last a lifetime!

This edition first published in 2015 by Bellwether Media, Inc.

No part of this publication may be reproduced in whole or in part without written permission of the publisher. For information regarding permission, write to Bellwether Media, Inc., Attention: Permissions Department, 5357 Penn Avenue South, Minneapolis, MN 55419.

Library of Congress Cataloging-in-Publication Data

Borgert-Spaniol, Megan, 1989-
  Black Bears / by Megan Borgert-Spaniol.
    pages cm. – (Blastoff! Readers. North American Animals)
  Includes bibliographical references and index.
  Summary: "Simple text and full-color photography introduce beginning readers to black bears. Developed by literacy experts for students in kindergarten through third grade"– Provided by publisher.
  ISBN 978-1-62617-186-2 (hardcover : alk. paper)
  1. Black bear–Juvenile literature. I. Title.
  QL737.C27B665 2015
  599.78'5–dc23
                        2014037332

Printed in the United States of America, North Mankato, MN.

# Table of Contents

# What Are Black Bears?

Black bears are the most common bears in North America. These **mammals** are found across Canada, the United States, and northern Mexico.

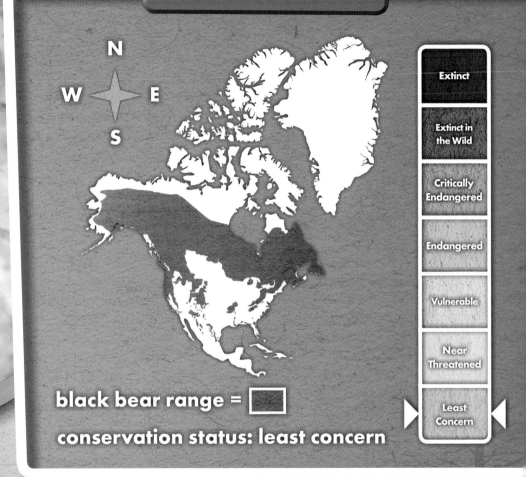

N
W E
S

black bear range = ☐

conservation status: least concern

Extinct

Extinct in the Wild

Critically Endangered

Endangered

Vulnerable

Near Threatened

Least Concern

Most black bears live in forests. Some make their homes in swamps, mountains, **scrublands**, and **tundra**.

## Identify a Black Bear

short claws
(1 to 2 inches)

tall ears

straight face
and nose

Not all black bears
are black. Those in
western areas often
have brownish fur.

Some black bears in the far north are blue-gray or creamy white.

average human

black bear

6

5

4

3

2

1

(feet)

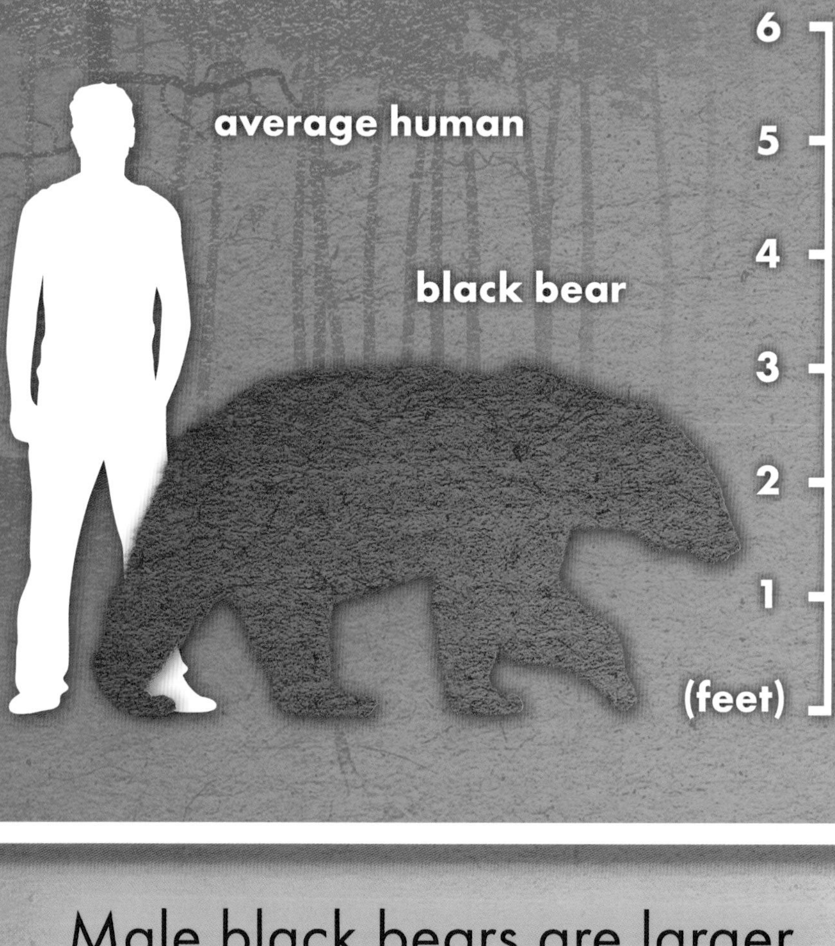

Male black bears are larger than females. Some measure more than 6 feet (1.8 meters) long. They can weigh more than 600 pounds (272 kilograms).

Black bears move quickly for their size. They can even climb trees with the help of their short, strong claws.

Black bears are **omnivores**. They mainly eat grasses, berries, nuts, and insects. They also dine on fish and **carrion**.

**acorns**

**beechnuts**

**bees**

**blueberries**

**hazelnuts**

**raspberries**

Black bears also like to eat food
left out by humans.

They find these snacks around campsites and hiking trails. This is dangerous for both the bears and humans.

# Summer to Spring

In summer, black bears
begin to eat large
amounts of food.

den

In fall, they gather leaves and twigs to build a nest in their **den**. This is how they prepare for winter.

In late fall, black bears start their **dormant** season.

They will sleep in their dens for six to seven months. They will not eat, drink, or exercise until spring.

## Mom and Cubs

In January, female black bears wake up to give birth. **Cubs** stay in their mom's den for several more months. They **nurse** while she sleeps.

## Baby Facts

Name for babies: cubs

Size of litter: 2 cubs
(most common)

Length of pregnancy: about 7 months

Time spent with mom: about 1.5 years

Mom and her cubs leave their den in spring. The cubs will stay with mom for another year.

She protects them as they learn to survive on their own!

# Glossary

**carrion**—the rotting meat of a dead animal

**cubs**—baby black bears

**den**—a sheltered place; black bears build dens underground, in caves, or in trees.

**dormant**—not active

**mammals**—warm-blooded animals that have backbones and feed their young milk

**nurse**—to drink mom's milk

**omnivores**—animals that eat both plants and animals

**scrublands**—dry lands with short bushes and trees

**tundra**—dry land where the ground is frozen year-round

# To Learn More

**AT THE LIBRARY**
Kolpin, Molly. *American Black Bears*. Mankato, Minn.: Capstone Press, 2012.

Magby, Meryl. *Black Bears*. New York, N.Y.: PowerKids Press, 2014.

Yolen, Jane. *Sleep, Black Bear, Sleep*. New York, N.Y.: HarperCollins, 2007.

**ON THE WEB**
Learning more about black bears is as easy as 1, 2, 3.

1. Go to www.factsurfer.com.

2. Enter "black bears" into the search box.

3. Click the "Surf" button and you will see a list of related web sites.

With factsurfer.com, finding more information is just a click away.

# Index